D1404464

TORNADOES

Dean Galiano

the rosen publishing group's
rosen central
new york

Published in 2000 by The Rosen Publishing Group, Inc.
29 East 21st Street, New York, NY 10010

First Edition

Galiano, Dean.
        Tornadoes / Dean Galiano.
                p.   cm. -- (Weather watchers' library)
        Includes bibliographical references and index.
        Summary: Analyzes tornadoes, including their origins, formation, intensity, destructive capabilities, and significance as a weather phenomenon.
        ISBN 0-8239-3094-7
        1. Tornadoes Juvenile literature. [1. Tornadoes.] I. Title.
II. Series: Galiano, Dean. Weather watchers' library.
        QC955.2.G35 1999
        551.55'3--dc21   99-33841
                                                                        CIP

Manufactured in the United States of America

CONTENTS

Introduction

The weather affects each of us every day. We often plan how to spend our time based on weather conditions. When it rains, we often choose to stay indoors. On the other hand, when it is warm and sunny, most of us put on our summer clothes and enjoy being outside. Many of the things that we own are designed for specific weather conditions. Our heavy jackets protect us from the cold of winter, and our umbrellas keep us from getting wet. The weather can even change the way we feel. Many people find rainy days drab and depressing, while others enjoy the wet weather. Most people love a warm, sunny day. In many ways, our lives actually revolve around the weather.

All of the weather that we experience takes place in something called the atmosphere. The atmosphere is a thin layer of air that surrounds Earth. When you look up into the huge sky, with its great masses of floating clouds, it is hard to think of the atmosphere as being small—but it really is. Weather actually happens in a very limited space. If Earth were shrunk to the size of a basketball, our atmosphere would be thinner than a piece of notebook paper.

Over the course of a year we experience all sorts of weather. Sometimes the weather is pleasant and warm, and sometimes it is cold and dreary. Depending on the season, either type of weather may be common. Occasionally, however, the weather gets extreme. So extreme, in fact, that weather becomes dangerous—even deadly!

Tornadoes are without question the most violent of all weather systems. Wind speeds in powerful tornadoes can reach up to 300 miles per hour. Under such conditions cars are picked up and thrown about like toys; huge freight trains are blown off their tracks; and entire buildings are picked up off the ground and torn apart in mid-air! That's how powerful tornadoes are.

1 Tornado Formation

What Is a Tornado?

A tornado is a rapidly spinning column of air that comes into contact with Earth's surface. We can't see air, but a tornado gathers clouds and dust with it as it moves, so we can see its shape. Tornadoes are almost always produced by one of two types of weather systems: severe thunderstorms or super-cell thunderstorms. Severe thunderstorms are capable of producing moderate-strength tornadoes, while supercell thunderstorms are super-powerful thunderstorms able to produce violent tornadoes.

As the whirling column of air descends from its parent thunderstorm, it forms a funnel cloud. Funnel clouds often do not reach the ground. These are called "funnels aloft." If the funnel does reach the ground, it is called a tornado.

A funnel cloud extends down from a storm mass to the ground.

Severe Thunderstorms

The vast majority of tornadoes are produced by severe thunderstorms. All thunderstorms are formed from cumulus clouds. These are the puffy white clouds that float gently across the summer sky. Cumulus clouds are formed when a mass of moist air comes into contact with a section of warm ground that has been heated by the sun. Contact with the ground warms the moist air. This warming makes the air lighter, so it floats upward into the atmosphere. As this warm, moist air rises into the atmosphere, it moves into areas where temperatures are lower. Eventually, the rising air cools to the dew point. The dew point is the temperature at which water vapor (water in the form of a gas) turns into a liquid through a process called condensation. The condensed water vapor forms water droplets, which are about a million times smaller than a single raindrop. These droplets are held in the air by the rising air mass and updrafts, or winds blowing up from the ground. The rising air then becomes visible as a cloud. As the cloud continues to grow and gather more moisture, the droplets collide and collect into larger and heavier droplets. Eventually these droplets become so heavy that the winds formed by the updraft can no

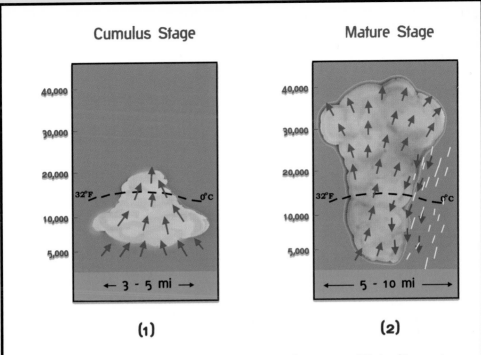

Cumulus Stage

Mature Stage

40,000
30,000
20,000
32°F — — — — 0°C
10,000
5,000
← 3 - 5 mi →

(1)

40,000
30,000
20,000
32°F — — — — 0°C
10,000
5,000
← 5 - 10 mi →

(2)

As a thunderhead moves from the cumulus stage (1) to its mature state as a cumulonimbus cloud (2), it grows rapidly.

longer hold the droplets in the air. At this point, the water falls from the cloud to the ground as precipitation—rain, snow, or sleet.

Severe thunderstorms develop when air conditions are unstable. Air becomes unstable when a mass of cold air comes into contact with a mass of much warmer air. Thunderheads, also called cumulonimbus clouds, form when air is unstable. Under these conditions, the higher the rising warm air mass travels in the atmosphere, the greater the temperature difference is between it and the surrounding air.

And if there is a great deal of moisture in the area, the cloud will continue to grow.

During spring and early summer, unstable air conditions are very common in the Midwestern United States. Warm, moist air drifting north from the Gulf of Mexico is trapped under a layer of dry air blown in from the deserts in Mexico and the American Southwest. With normal thunderstorm formation, warm, moist air rises higher and higher into the atmosphere to form clouds. In this case, however, the layer of dry air acts as a cap that prevents the warm, moist air from rising beyond the dry air layer. This cap prevents the normal formation of moderate-sized thunderstorms. Instead, the warm, moist air builds up extreme levels of air pressure because there is nowhere for that rising air to go. Meanwhile, high in the atmosphere, above the dry desert air, a layer of extremely cold air makes the air conditions even more unstable. This is because these two pressure systems are pushing against each other. When the instability becomes too great, the moist, tropical air bursts up through the cap of dry air. As if it were a bathtub drain pointing up at the sky, the puncture sucks up masses of warm, moist air from miles around. This warm air reacts quickly and violently with the upper

Under specific conditions, such as wind direction, this threatening cloud formation can become a tornado.

cold air mass. This reaction creates thunderheads at a much more rapid rate than they would normally be produced—and a severe thunderstorm is born.

Tornado Alley

Although tornadoes occur in many places throughout the world, most of them take place in the United States. At one time or another, every continental U.S. state, from Alabama to Alaska, has been struck by a tornado. Most of the tornadoes that occur in the United States take place in the Midwest. One area in particular, known as "Tornado Alley," experiences a great deal of tornado activity. Tornado Alley stretches from eastern Texas, northward through Oklahoma, Kansas, Iowa, and Nebraska. It's not so much the location as the topography, or the shape of the land, that has created Tornado Alley. If a tornado is going to strike anywhere in the country, chances are good that it will occur in Tornado Alley. The heavy tornado activity in this area is a result of the large number of severe thunderstorms that happen here.

Supercell Thunderstorms

Supercell thunderstorms develop from severe thunderstorms when changing wind directions at different heights in the atmosphere cause the updraft into the storm to rotate. An updraft is a collection of warm, moist air blowing up into a cloud from Earth's surface.

The updraft is what fuels a thunderstorm and keeps it going. The stronger the updraft, the more intense the thunderstorm.

The rotating updraft itself is called a mesocyclone. In a non-supercell thunderstorm, a cool wind— called a downdraft—coming from the base of the storm itself soon cuts off the updraft that fuels the storm. In a super-cell, however, the updraft rotates so that the normal downdraft is not effective in cutting off its supply of warm, moist air. Now the storm can last much longer than a non-super-cell thunderstorm.

As a supercell rises in the atmos-phere, its mesocy-clone stretches up-ward. The higher the supercell rises and stretches into

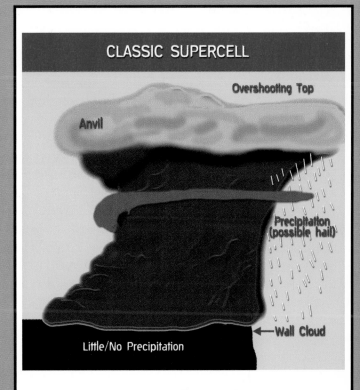

CLASSIC SUPERCELL

Overshooting Top

Anvil

Precipitation (possible hail)

Little/No Precipitation

←Wall Cloud

Supercell thunderstorms have a particular shape to them.

Wall Clouds

A wall cloud is a circular cloud that often forms around the base of a mesocyclone. It is usually about two miles across. Wall clouds form in the updrafts of mesocyclones. As the updraft draws moist, rain-cooled air into the system, the air begins to condense at a height lower than that of the cloud base. This creates a cloud that starts close to the ground and rises upward, making it look as if a wall has formed.

Wall clouds have a frightening appearance, but not all wall clouds form tornadoes. Those that do usually appear ten to twenty minutes before the tornado is seen. The wall cloud begins to rotate steadily, and then violently, just before the tornado appears.

the upper atmosphere, the faster the mesocyclone spins. It is from this rapidly spinning mesocyclone that most damaging tornadoes develop.

At this point the spinning mesocyclone needs two more things to happen to produce a tornado. First, the dry air that earlier acted as a cap must flow into the downdraft of the supercell. This strengthens the downdraft. Second, the cool, downrushing air from the downdraft must mix with the warm, humid air of the updraft. This usually occurs when a southeast surface wind mixes with an upper-air southwest or west wind. Now the cool, dry air from the downdraft mixes in with the updraft. It makes the air rotate even faster. This can provide the necessary

This mesocyclone gets its shape from the circular winds that rotate the storm.

"kick" to create a tornado in the mesocyclone. The balance of the updraft and the downdraft must be just right for a tornado to occur. Only very rarely is the balance just right. This is why out of hundreds of thunderstorms, only a small percentage will produce tornadoes.

In a supercell thunderstorm that produces a tornado, the mesocyclone narrows and spirals down out of the thundercloud with the cool, dry air from the downdraft. The water vapor in the spinning column of air condenses, and a funnel cloud appears. As the funnel cloud narrows, its rotation increases to incredibly high speeds.

2 Funnel Clouds and Tornadoes

Sometimes funnel clouds are very distinct; sometimes they are barely visible. If the funnel reaches the ground, it becomes a tornado. As tornadoes move forward, they suck up dust and debris from the ground. With all of these particles swirling around in its column of air, the tornado darkens in color and its shape becomes well-defined.

Funnel Cloud Shapes and Sizes

Tornado funnels form in several different shapes. Sometimes the funnel becomes wider at the bottom than at the top. At other times funnels are shaped like cylinders or hourglasses. Sometimes they are shaped like long ropes, or long twisting columns.

The typical funnel is about 800 to 2,000 feet tall. Some funnels extend downward from the clouds, but never reach the ground. Others may touch the ground many different times, disappearing back

Funnel clouds appear in different shapes and sizes.

17

into the clouds in between touchdowns. Most tornado funnels are less than a mile wide at their bases, the point at which the tip touches the ground. The average width at the ground is about 200 to 300 yards, but some are as small as ten feet wide at their tip. Because their tips are narrow, the damage from tornadoes is limited to narrow paths along the ground. Thus, as a tornado moves through a town it may destroy one house completely, while leaving the house next door undamaged.

Movement of Tornadoes

Tornadoes move forward at speeds of up to seventy miles per hour. Sometimes they may hover over one spot for several minutes. The typical tornado, however, moves along at about twenty to forty miles per hour. Most tornadoes travel diagonally, from the southwest to the northeast, but a small number of tornadoes are capable of approaching a location from any direction.

The path of a weak tornado—with wind speeds reaching only 72 miles per hour—is typically less than one mile long and fewer than 100 yards wide. A weak tornado has a life expectancy of only one to three minutes. A strong tornado, however—with wind speeds greater than 113 miles per hour—can leave a path of destruction over 100 miles long and hundreds of yards wide. Very strong tornadoes can last for over two hours. Wind speeds in these powerful tornadoes are estimated to reach up to 300 miles per hour.

The destructive force of a tornado is limited to the narrow path that its tip travels along on the ground.

Caught in a Tornado!

Strangely enough, there have been cases reported of people who have found themselves right in the vortex—the swirling center—of a tornado. In some cases, people have had their houses torn apart around them without being injured themselves. As these people watched the funnel cloud pass overhead, they observed some very eerie things take place. A Kansas farmer reported seeing his cast-iron stove circling over his head. Other people have reported having their clothes ripped off by the wind. One man in Alabama stated that, "although the tornado was not directly overhead, our home was lifted up and down at least a dozen times."

Multi-vortex Tornadoes

Multi-vortex tornadoes are usually the most destructive of all tornadoes. These tornadoes have more than one funnel. These mini-funnels, called vortices, revolve around a common center. Dust, debris, and clouds often make it difficult to see the individual vortices. Multi-vortex tornadoes are very large, and because they have more than one funnel, they leave a wider path of destruction than single-vortex tornadoes.

3 When Tornadoes Strike

Tornadoes are dangerous to people and property, mainly because of their strong winds. In violent tornadoes the updraft near the center of the storm's funnel may reach 100 miles per hour. These high-powered updrafts allow a tornado to produce winds of up to 300 miles per hour. These winds can blow down trees and telephone poles, and have enough force to pick up entire train cars or even lift a house off its foundation. Flying debris causes many of the deaths and much of the damage associated with tornadoes. Broken glass, tree limbs, and even objects as heavy as cars and trucks become airborne missiles. Imagine a car flying through the air and slamming into your home at 100 miles per hour!

The F-Scale

The F-Scale classifies tornadoes according to their wind speeds. The scale is named for Professor T.

This upended home is undoubtedly the result of a category F3 or F4 tornado.

Theodore Fujita of the University of Chicago, who created it. By studying the amount and type of property damage, Fujita estimated the wind speeds of various tornadoes. The scale ranges from F0 (a weak tornado) to F5 (an incredibly strong tornado).

An F0 tornado causes only minor damage, such as snapping twigs off trees and breaking some windows. F1 and F2 tornadoes can cause more damage. The winds they produce can tear the shingles off of roofs, push cars around, and demolish mobile homes. An F3 tornado can tear roofs off of well-built homes and overturn entire trains. An F4 tornado has wind speeds high enough to destroy whole buildings and throw cars through the air like toys. An F5 tornado, the strongest of all, has enough power to pick up a sturdy building and tear it apart in mid-air!

Fortunately, F5 tornadoes do not occur very often. Of the hundreds of tornadoes that strike the United States every year, only one or two will be rated an F5. When an F5 tornado does strike, however, it leaves total destruction in its path. In June 1984, an F5 tornado hit the small town of Barneveld, Wisconsin. In less than a minute, it completely destroyed more than 100 homes and killed nine people.

As a tornado makes its way across the ground, its rating on the F-Scale can go up or down. A tornado that originally hits the ground as an F1 or an F2 can gain strength and develop into an F3, F4, or even an F5.

It is estimated that in an average year, 79 percent of all tornadoes are weak, 20 percent are strong, and only about 1 percent are violent. It is these few violent tornadoes, however, that cause the greatest amount of destruction and the most deaths. On average, tornadoes kill nearly eighty people every year. They also injure about 1,500 people.

Outbreaks

Most tornadoes, even the very powerful ones, are usually small, don't last very long, and often occur in unpopulated areas. On rare occasions, however, multiple tornadoes strike together in a tornado outbreak. In April 1974, an outbreak of 148 tornadoes tore through thirteen states in the east-central United States. This "super outbreak" raced across the land for more than fifteen hours. By the time it was over, the tornadoes had killed 315 people and caused more than $600 million in damage.

The F-Scale

F-Scale	Tornado Intensity
F0	Gale Tornado
F1	Moderate Tornado
F2	Significant Tornado
F3	Severe Tornado
F4	Devastating Tornado
F5	Incredible Tornado

Wind Speeds	Type of Damage
40–72 mph	Some damage to chimneys; breaks branches off trees; pushes over shallow-rooted trees; damages sign boards.
73–112 mph	Peels surfaces off roads; pushes mobile homes off foundations or overturns them; pushes moving autos off roads; may destroy attached garages.
113–157 mph	Tears roofs off frame houses; demolishes mobile homes; snaps or uproots large trees; generates light-object missiles.
158–206 mph	Tears roofs and some walls off well-constructed houses; overturns trains; uproots most trees in forests.
207–260 mph	Levels well-constructed houses; blows away structures with foundations some distance; throws some cars and generates large missiles.
261–318 mph	Lifts strong frame houses off foundations; carries away considerable-sized missiles through the air distances in excess of 300 feet; debarks trees; badly damages steel-reinforced concrete structures.

Damage to Structures

For a long time it was thought that tornadoes caused buildings to explode. This misconception was based on the idea that there were differences in air pressure between the tornado and the inside of a building. Air pressure is the weight of air in the atmosphere pressing down on any one spot. It was assumed that the relative air pressure in a building could not adjust fast enough to the very low air pressure of a tornado. People thought that this air pressure imbalance was responsible for the

The most sturdy room in the house, like a bathroom, often survives a violent tornado.

destruction of some buildings that appeared to have exploded as the tornado came upon them.

When tornadoes were detected, people were told to open a window in their homes. It was believed that doing this would make the air pressures inside and outside the house equal, preventing the house from exploding. It is now known, however, that most buildings have enough air leaks in them to prevent indoor air pressures from ever becoming explosive.

During a tornado, most buildings are actually damaged in one of two ways. They are either struck with flying debris or they have their roofs lifted off, which often causes the walls to collapse. The lifting of roofs is caused by strong air currents blowing across the tops of buildings. This pulls at the roof joints with such force that many roof structures are unable to hold together.

Tornadoes are usually accompanied by heavy downpours of rain and hail that can also cause damage. The heavy showers usually fall before the tornado hits. They sometimes obscure the tornado itself from sight. Hailstones as large as softballs have been reported just before a tornado strikes. Hailstones of this size are the result of a thunderstorm with an incredibly strong updraft.

4 Studying Tornadoes

For years, scientists have tried to better understand the structure of tornadoes and how they develop. Until very recently, they met with little success. Traditional weather instruments—gauges measuring temperature, pressure, wind, and humidity (the amount of water in the air)—have been of little use, as they are not strong enough to withstand the high winds that tornadoes produce.

Storm-Chasers

In the spring of 1994 and 1995, a daring scientific project, called VORTEX, was conducted by a group of scientists. Using specially designed cars, the scientists drove to various points around supercell thunderstorms. They took readings of the temperature, humidity, and wind. One of the vehicles actually had its own specialized radar system. This specialized radar was used to scan

Before meteorologists used radar and satellite imagery to help forecast the weather, meteorology was very low-tech.

Doppler Radar and Tornadoes

Radar (which stands for Radio Detection and Ranging) sends high-frequency radio waves into the air that are much higher than what are used for AM and FM radio. When these radio waves hit something that's in the air, like an airplane or flock of birds, the waves bounce off it and return to the radar. These returning waves produce an image on a television screen that highlights the airborne object. Radar was developed during World War II to detect approaching enemy aircraft. While scanning the sky for enemy planes, the radar operators made the discovery that they could also detect clouds and precipitation—rain, snow, and hail.

Electronic weather maps (opposite page) are made possible by radar units (this page) that capture images of clouds and precipitation as they travel across Earth.

the wind structures of storms. In addition, two jet planes scanned the tops of the storms with their own Doppler radar systems.

Towards the end of the project, in June 1995, VORTEX detected several violent tornadoes in west Texas. The information that was gathered from these tornadoes has been very valuable in adding to what we already know about tornadoes.

Today meteorologists use radar to detect the location and strength of storm systems by tracking the movements of rain, snow, and hail. Precipitation reflects the radio waves to the radar station at different frequencies (waves of sound or light). The frequency is determined by whether the wind is blowing the precipitation away from or toward the radar station. This change in frequency is called the "Doppler effect," named for the man who first discovered its features, Christian Johann Doppler, in 1842. You can experience the Doppler effect when you listen to the sound of a car driving by as you stand still on the side of a street. As the car passes, the sound it makes decreases in frequency. You hear a lower-pitched sound from an object heading away from you than one heading toward you.

In the 1970s meteorologists began testing radar that could detect the Doppler effect caused by wind-blown precipitation. Doppler radar allows meteorologists to see the swirling winds inside thunderstorms. Since these winds may lead to a tornado, early detection means the authorities can issue an earlier tornado warning to the public.

Storm-Spotters

In communities where severe weather happens often, some people volunteer to become "storm-spotters." Storm-spotters are trained by the National Weather Service. Their job is to watch for weather that may lead to severe thunderstorm activity. Storm-spotters telephone in sightings of thunder-storm systems and funnel cloud formations to area weather stations. The work that storm-spotters do helps meteorologists to issue severe weather warn-ings earlier—possibly saving lives.

5) Tornado Safety

The chances that you will experience a tornado are small. Even in areas of the United States where tornado activity is common, a tornado is not likely to strike any one place more than once every 250 years. However, since tornadoes are potential killers, it is good to know some safety rules in case you experience a tornado.

The National Weather Service issues a tornado warning when a tornado has been spotted. When a tornado warning is issued, it will be broadcast by local television and radio stations. In urban areas, tornado sirens will sound, as well. When a tornado warning is issued, or if you see a funnel cloud approaching, the most important thing to do is find shelter immediately. Depending on where you are at the time, the following list explains where to go:

⊙ In office buildings: Go to an interior hallway on the lowest floor, or to the designated shelter area.

Tornadoes sometimes leave total destruction where they hit.

⊙ In shopping centers: Go to a designated shelter area. Do not go to your parked car.

⊙ In homes: The basement is the safest place. Seek shelter under sturdy furniture if possible. In homes without basements, take cover in the center of the house, on the lowest floor, in a small room such as a closet or bathroom. Stay as far away from windows as possible.

Bathrooms are often the safest rooms in a house during a tornado because they are small, with few or no windows.

⊙ Mobile homes: These are very vulnerable to destructive winds. Proper tie-downs to prevent overturning will minimize damage. Do not stay in the mobile home during a tornado warning. Go to a designated community shelter. If there are no shelters, seek refuge in a well-constructed building. If there is no well-constructed building nearby, seek shelter in a ditch or ravine that is not flooded. The idea is to get as low to the ground as possible.

⊙ In schools: Your school should have a safety procedure and practice it with tornado drills. If not,

Schools have safety plans to protect students from injury during violent storms.

avoid auditoriums and gymnasiums that have high, wide, unstable roofs, and go to an interior hallway on the lowest floor.

⊙ In open country: If there is no time to find suitable shelter, lie flat in the nearest and deepest depression, such as a ditch or ravine.

It is a good idea to keep a portable, battery-operated radio in your home. Listen to this during the tornado warning. Your local radio networks will inform you when the danger is over. It is also a good idea to have some flashlights on hand in case the power goes out.

Glossary

air pressure The weight of an air mass in the atmosphere pressing down on any one spot.

atmosphere The thin layer of air surrounding Earth.

condensation The process in which water vapor (water in the form of a gas) turns into a liquid.

cumulonimbus clouds Puffy, gray clouds that form vertically, and usually produce storms; also called thunderheads.

cumulus clouds Puffy white clouds associated with fair weather.

Doppler effect A change in frequency (waves of sound or light) depending on movement toward or away from an object.

Doppler radar Radar that detects and measures precipitation (such as rain, snow, or hail).

downdraft A quick flow of downward-moving air from the atmosphere.

F-Scale A measurement scale that classifies tornadoes according to their wind speeds.

funnel aloft A funnel cloud whose tail never touches the ground.

funnel cloud A rapidly spinning cloud in the form of a funnel but not yet touching the ground.

humidity The amount of measured water in the air.

mesocyclone The rotating updraft of a supercell thunderstorm.

multi-vortex tornado A tornado that has two or more funnel clouds touching the ground that spin around a shared center point.

National Weather Service A government agency responsible for observing and forecasting weather.

RADAR The acronym for Radio Detection And Ranging. This instrument is used to find far-off objects by transmitting radio waves into the air to bounce off the objects and return to the machine as reflections of that airborne object.

supercell thunderstorm An especially powerful thunderstorm that is a single mass.

tornado A rapidly spinning column of air that comes into contact with the ground.

unstable air mass Rising air that is greatly different in temperature from the air around it.

updraft Strong vertical winds that flow up from the ground into clouds.

water vapor Water in the form of a gas.

For Further Reading

Allaby, Michael. *Tornadoes*. New York: Facts on File, 1997.

Davies-Jones, Robert. "Tornadoes." *Scientific American*, August 1995.

Ehrlbach, Arlene. *Tornadoes*. Danbury, CT: Children's Press, 1994.

Greenberg, Keith. *Hurricanes and Tornadoes*. New York: Twenty-First Century Books, 1995.

Herman, Gail. *Storm Chasers: Tracking Twisters*. New York: Putnam, 1997.

Kahl, Jonathan D. *Storm Warning! The Power of Tornadoes and Hurricanes*. Minneapolis: Lerner Publishing Group, 1993.

Lampton, Christopher. *Tornado* (A Disaster Book). Brookfield, CT: Millbrook Press, 1998.

Meister, Carl. *Tornadoes*. Minneapolis: ABDO Publishing, 1998.

Rose, Sally. *Tornadoes*. New York: Simon and Schuster's Children, 1999.

Rotter, Charles. *Tornadoes*. New York: Creative Education, 1997.

Simon, Seymour. *Tornadoes*. New York: Morrow Junior, 1999.

Resources

ORGANIZATIONS

National Oceanic and Atmospheric Administration
United States Department of Commerce
14th Street and Constitution Avenue NW
Room 6013
Washington, DC 20230
(202) 482-6090
Web site: http://www.noaa.gov
e-mail: webmaster@www.noaa.gov

National Weather Service
1325 East-West Highway
Room 18454
Silver Spring, MD 20910
Web site: http://www.nws.noaa.gov
e-mail: w-nws.webmaster@noaa.gov

Tornado Project
P.O. Box 302
St. Johnsbury, VT 05819
Web site: http://www.tornadoproject.com
e-mail: tornproj@plainfield.bypass.com

Tornado and Storm Research Organisation
Attn: Prof. Derek Elsom
Geography Department
Oxford Brookes University
Gipsy Lane

Headington, Oxford, Oxfordshire, U.K.
OX3 0BP
Web site: http://www.torro.org.uk
e-mail: dmelsom@brookes.ac.uk
This organization is in the United Kingdom, which has the highest frequency of reported tornadoes per unit area in the world.

WEB SITES

Fact Sheet: Tornadoes
Web site: http://www.fema.gov/library/tornadof.htm
Advanced planning and quick response tips for surviving a tornado, from the Federal Emergency Management Agency (FEMA).

USA Today: Tornadoes
Web site:
http://www.usatoday.com/weather/tornado/wtwist0.htm
The latest details on tornado formation and research.

Scientific American Explorations: Turn! Turn! Turn!
Web site: http://www.sciam.com/explorations/
052096explorations.html
Scientists unravel the twisted ways of tornadoes.

Index

Credits

About the Author

Dean Galiano is a freelance writer. He lives in New York City.

Photo Credits

Cover, Title Page ©Paul & Linda Marie Ambrose/FPG; pp. 6-7 © J. Kuckerman/Corbis/Westlight; p.11 © Clyde H. Smith/FPG; p.15,16-17 ©Charles Doswell III/Tony Stone; p.19 ©Warren Faidley/International Stock; pp.20-21,21(funnel clouds) ©Faildey, Agliolo/International Stock; p.20 ©Jim Rogash/AP Wide World; p.21 ©Galen Rowell/Corbis; pp.22-23 © Hulton Getty/Tony Stone; p.28 ©Jonathan Blair/Corbis; pp.30-31 ©Cobis/Hulton-Deutsch Collection; pp.32-33 ©Chip Simons/FPG; p.32 ©Mark Gibson/Corbis; pp.36-37 ©Corbis/AFP; p.38 ©Alan McGee/FPG; p.39 © Pauline Cutler/Tony Stone; pp.9,13 Illustrations by Lisa Quattlebaum.

Cover Design

Kim M. Sonsky

Book Design and Layout

Lisa Quattlebaum

Consulting Editors

Mark Beyer and Jennifer Ceaser